Walking Together
IN THE FREEDOM SQUARE OF VICTORY

The Journey of Dr John Garang and South Sudan

BY DAVID JOCK NHIAL

A Note from the Publisher

The publisher wishes to acknowledge and thank Dr Douglas H. Johnson for his invaluable help and support for Africa World Books and its mission of preserving and promoting African cultural and literary traditions and history. Dr Johnson and fellow historians have been instrumental in ensuring that African people remain connected to their past and their identity. Africa World Books is proud to carry on this mission.

Graphic Design by Bronwyn Parker
Edited by Rosemary Purcell
Published by Africa World Books

Acknowledgements

Very gratefully, I thank exceptional Friend Emmanuel Atem for supervising and advising on the importance of the Children's edition. I thank everyone on the scribe teams who helped me during information gathering. Thanks to those who encouraged or taught me something about Dr John Garang and our nation.

Many thanks to Rosemary Purcell, the Editor. Thanks also to Graphic Designers Bronwyn Parker and Andrew McDonough - Publishing Skill, I am grateful to Hon James Hoth Mai, Minister for Labour, for linking me with the family of Dr John Garang.

I recognise Mabil Ajak and Monyak Ajak for the coordination and particular appreciation to NyanKuir John Garang, - Daughter of Dr John Garang, for her immense support.

Table of Contents

Look up all the great info here!

List of figures

Want to find a picture? Check out these...

About the author

David Jock was one of the Lost Boys from southern Sudan. He walked to Ethiopia when he was nine. He stayed there for two years. He had to return to Sudan when the Ethiopian Government changed.

David spent eleven years in Kakuma Refugee camp in Kenya and attended school and came to Australia on humanitarian visas and settle in Adelaide. David studies hard to become a social worker. He has an Associate Degree of Arts in Youth Work, a Bachelor of Arts, a Post Graduate Certificate in Child Wellbeing and a Master of Social Work. David now works with the Youth sector. In 2012, David was a finalist in the Pride of Australia Medals

Cover note

This book is for South Sudanese children in Australia. It will help them learn about the history of John Garang, the founding father of South Sudan. It is also for all children who are interested in how South Sudan became the world's newest country.

Until 2011, northern Sudan and South Sudan were one country (the Republic of Sudan). South Sudan separated from Sudan after many years of war.

About two million people were killed by the end of this war. Many belonged to southern Sudanese ethnic groups. Most people in South Sudan are Christian. Most people in the north (now called Sudan) are Muslim. Dr Garang worked with the southern rebels in this war.

South Sudan became independent on 11 July 2011.

Image Credit: St Columba College South Australia

Dr. John Garang de Mabior

Foreword

**John Garang de Mabior Atem was born on 23 June 1945.
His home was in Buk village, in the Bor area of Jonglei, southern Sudan.**

His parents were Mabior Atem and Gak Malwal Kuol. (The Dinka are one of the largest ethnic groups in southern Sudan.) He was the sixth of the family's ten children – seven boys and three girls. His parents were strict Christians. Sadly, they died when he was ten.

This book is about John Garang's contribution to southern Sudan. It helps to explain why he is a hero to southern Sudanese people.

John Garang was the founder of the Sudan People's Liberation Movement. This movement is also known as the SPLM. He also founded the Sudan Liberation Army. This army is also known as the SLA.

John Garang became the Vice President of the Republic of Sudan and the President of the government of southern Sudan on 9 July 2005. He signed a peace treaty with the government in northern Sudan to end one of Africa's longest wars. He died in a helicopter crash three weeks later, on 30 July 2005. He was travelling from Uganda to southern Sudan. He was sixty.

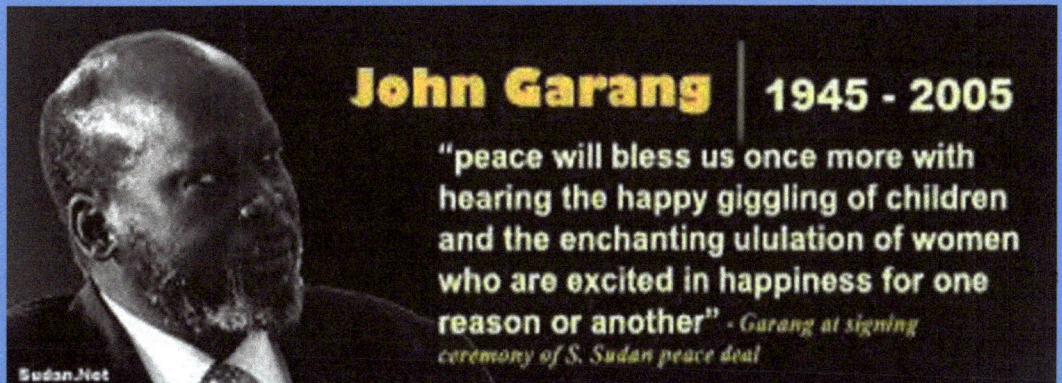

John Garang | **1945 - 2005**

"peace will bless us once more with hearing the happy giggling of children and the enchanting ululation of women who are excited in happiness for one reason or another" - *Garang at signing ceremony of S. Sudan peace deal*

Sudan.Net

x

PART 1

The first part of this book is a short history
of Sudan from 1946 to 2011,
when South Sudan became a country.

It concentrates on the contribution made
by Dr John Garang.

It also includes information about South Sudan today.

Independence

For many years, southern and northern Sudan were governed separately. The north and the south have cultural and religious differences.

The north was originally settled by Arab tribes from Egypt. People in the south were African ethnic groups.

These differences caused conflicts. Conflict was also caused by other countries taking control of Sudan.

In 1946, the north and the south were merged into one region. Arabic became the official language.

Sudan gained full independence on 1 January 1956. The new government was based in Khartoum (in the north). Most of the politicians were people from the north. They encouraged economic development in the north, along the irrigated valley of the River Nile.

The government wanted Muslim policies and customs. The people in the south were not happy. They wanted to run their own region themselves. They wanted to have their share of economic development. They wanted to use their own languages in their schools.

In 1956, the south rebelled against the government in Khartoum, starting the First Sudanese Civil War. It was led by the Anya Nya rebel army.

The First Sudanese Civil War (1956-1972)

The First Sudanese Civil War was between the southern Anya Nya 1 movement and the government in the north. It lasted seventeen years.

Joseph Lagu was the first leader of Anya Nya I. He was born on 21 November 1931 in southern Sudan. He was from the Madi ethnic group. He joined the Sudanese Army in 1960.

General Lagu joined the Southern Sudan Resistance Movement in June 1963. He led the Ana Nya 1. Anya Nya is the Madi term for snake or scorpion venom. The rebels had been fighting for independence from the Sudanese Government since the start of the war in 1956.

Figure 1: Joseph Lagu, the first leader of Anya Nya 1

John Garang joined Anya Nya 1 in 1962. But he was only seventeen, so he kept studying. By 1969, he had a Bachelor of Arts degree in Economics from the United States.

He re-joined Anya Nya I in 1971. He went to a company commanders' course at the American Military Academy, where he graduated in the top three. He remained in the army until he left Sudan for his doctoral studies in the United States.

The First Sudanese Civil War ended in 1972. General Lagu and the Sudanese president, Gaafar Mohamed el Nimeiri, signed the Addis Ababa Agreement. This agreement gave the people of the south more power over their own affairs.

Figure 2: John Garang as a young man

The years between wars

Figure 3:
Colonel John
Garang

Figure 4:
John Garang

The Addis Ababa Agreement gave independence to the south. Rebel fighters, like John Garang, became part of the Sudanese Army. He was promoted to Colonel and sent to the United States for training.

A few years later, in 1976, John Garang married Rebecca Nyandeng in Juba, Sudan. They also had a traditional ceremony in their village.

In 1978, John Garang and his wife went to the United States. He continued his studies. He graduated with a PhD in Economics in 1981.

De Mabior receiving his doctorate (PhD) from Iowa State University, United States of America

After his graduation, Dr Garang returned to Sudan. He was appointed Deputy Director of Military Research and commander of an infantry battalion in Khartoum.

Figure 5: John Garang and his wife Rebecca and baby

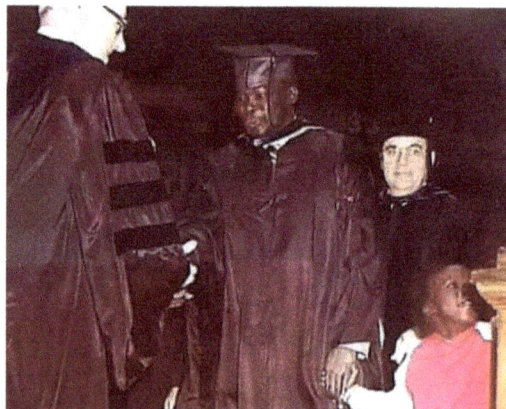

Figure 6: Rare photo of Dr John Garang

The Second Sudanese Civil War (1983-2005)

Unfortunately, the Addis Ababa Agreement did not last long. There were a few reasons.

In 1978, oil was discovered in southern Sudan. President Gaafar Nimeiri wanted to control the oil fields so the south didn't get the money for it. Islamic law was introduced in the early 1980s. Northern Arabs used black slavery. Arabic became the official language at schools.

On 16 May 1983, a group of army officers based at Bor mutinied. Dr Garang was sent by President Nimeiri to stop the mutiny. Instead, he joined the anti-government rebels in Ethiopia. He then became the leader of this group, known as Anya Nya II.

Anya Nya II was split into the Sudan People's Liberation Movement (SPLM), and the Sudan People's Liberation Army (SPLA). Dr Garang became the Chairman of SPLM and the Commander-in-Chief of SPLA.

Dr Garang encouraged other army forces to mutiny against Islamic law. This mutiny was the beginning of the Second Sudanese Civil War. The war resulted in many deaths.

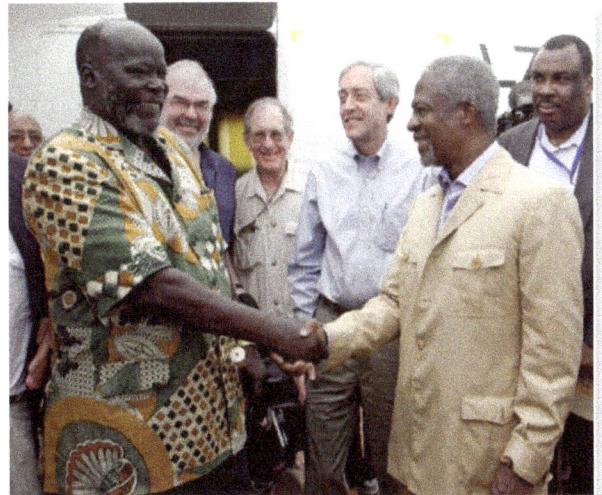

Figure 7: John Garang greeting former UN secretary general Kofi Annan

As the poster below shows, Dr Garang wanted proper buildings and roads.

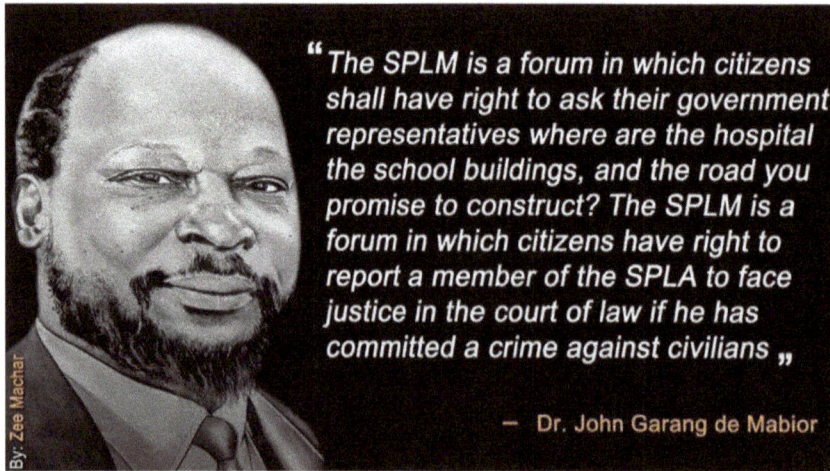

"The SPLM is a forum in which citizens shall have right to ask their government representatives where are the hospital the school buildings, and the road you promise to construct? The SPLM is a forum in which citizens have right to report a member of the SPLA to face justice in the court of law if he has committed a crime against civilians"

— Dr. John Garang de Mabior

By: Zee Machar

Figure 8: Sudan People's Liberation Movement poster

Libya, Uganda and Ethiopia backed the SPLA. Dr Garang and his army controlled a large part of the southern regions of the country, named New Sudan. He said their courage came from 'the conviction that we are fighting a just cause. That is something North Sudan and its people don't have.'

Up to two million soldiers and civilians died during this war. Over seven million people were displaced from their homes or became refugees in neighbouring countries. Today, hundreds of thousands of Sudanese people still live in refugee camps, waiting to go home.

Figure 9: Dr Garang leading the rebels

In 1985, President Nimeiri was dismissed. Islamic law was abolished by the new government. However, Dr Garang remained a rebel leader.

In 1991 there was a revolution in Ethiopia (Sudan's neighbour, and where millions of people were living in refugee camps). Ethiopia had supported the SPLA. Sudanese refugees were forced to return to Sudan. Islamic law was re-introduced, but not applied to all southern states.

There was also conflict between various ethnic groups in southern Sudan.

In 1999, Sudan began to export oil. There was a problem though. While most of the oil was in the south, the oil refineries were in the north.

The president of Sudan, President Umar al-Bashir, and Dr Garang held peace talks in 2001. However, they failed.

The Sudanese Government and the SPLA signed the Machakos Protocol in 2002 to end the civil war. The Sudanese Government accepted the right of the south to seek self-determination after a six-year interim period.

A week later, on 27 July 2002, President Al-Bashir and SPLA leader Dr Garang met face-to-face for the first time The Ugandan president, Yoweri Museveni, helped make this happen.

In October 2002, the Sudanese Government and the SPLA agreed to a ceasefire while negotiations were taking place. This did not stop the fighting.

Those negotiations stopped in November 2002. The government and the SPLA couldn't agree about who should get government jobs.

The Sudanese Government and the SPLA agreed to a power-sharing arrangement in 2004 as part of a peace deal to end the civil war.

Figure 10: John Garang with South Sudanese president Omar Bashir after brokering a peace deal

The Second Sudanese Civil War (1983-2005) cont.

The war finally ended when the SPLA and the government signed a peace agreement on 9 January 2005 in Nairobi, Kenya.

As part of the peace agreement, on 9 July 2005 Dr Garang was sworn in as the first person from southern Sudan to hold the position of Vice President of the Republic of Sudan. This made him the second most powerful person in the country. President Omer Hassan Ahmed el-Beshir also appointed him President of the Government of Southern Sudan. No Christian or southerner had ever held such a high government post. Commenting after the ceremony, Dr Garang said, 'I congratulate the Sudanese people, this is not my peace or the peace of al-Bashir, it is the peace of the Sudanese people'.

Figure 11: Dr Garang is sworn in as Vice President of Sudan (Photo Source: news.bbc.co.uk)

Dr John Garang died in a helicopter crash on 30 July 2005 in Eastern Equatoria. He was returning from an official visit to Uganda. He was survived by his wife Rebecca and their six children: two boys and four girls.

Southern Sudan, and the whole of Sudan, had lost its beloved son, Dr John Garang de Mabior.

Figure 12: John Garang boarding the helicopter (Photo Source: news.bbc.co.uk)

Figure 13: US President George W Bush meets Rebecca Garang, Minister of Transportation, Roads and Bridges of the Government of South Sudan, in the Oval Office of the White House in Washington, 10 February 2006 (Reuters). (White House photo by Eric Draper, Public domain, via Wikimedia Commons).

Condolence messages from world leaders

The world was shocked to hear of the death of Dr Garang. Below are some of the condolence messages, expressing hope that his death would not obstruct the peace process.

'We are confident that the peace agreement will proceed as it was planned and drawn up and that the future of Sudan will remain a trust in our hearts and the hearts of the brothers in the [SPLM] movement.'
Sudanese President Omar Hassan al-Bashir

'He was a visionary leader and peacemaker who helped bring about the comprehensive peace agreement, which is a beacon of hope for all Sudanese ... John Garang's vision of peace must be embraced by all the people in Sudan so that they can live in a democratic, peaceful and united country.'
US President George W Bush

'It is with great shock and sadness that the Government and people of South Africa learned of the death of Dr John Garang de Mabior, the first Vice President of the Republic of [the] Sudan.
'It is especially tragic that Dr Garang's death comes a mere three weeks after his inauguration as the first Vice President of the Republic of the Sudan on 9 July 2005.'
South Africa's President Thabo Mbeki

'Dr Garang was one of the most visionary and incisive revolutionary thinkers and nationalists Africa has ever produced.'
– UN Secretary General Kofi Annan

Condolence messages from world leaders cont.

'I do appreciate that the new-found peace in Sudan was inextricably interwoven with the very person of Dr Garang. I, however, express the hope and optimism that every effort will be taken to ensure that the physical absence of Dr Garang will not in any way jeopardise the gains made towards durable peace.'

Kenya's President Mwai Kibaki

'If they [Sudanese people] loved him, they should remain calm and carry on with his vision. It is John Garang who is dead. The vision should be kept alive.'

Rebecca Garang

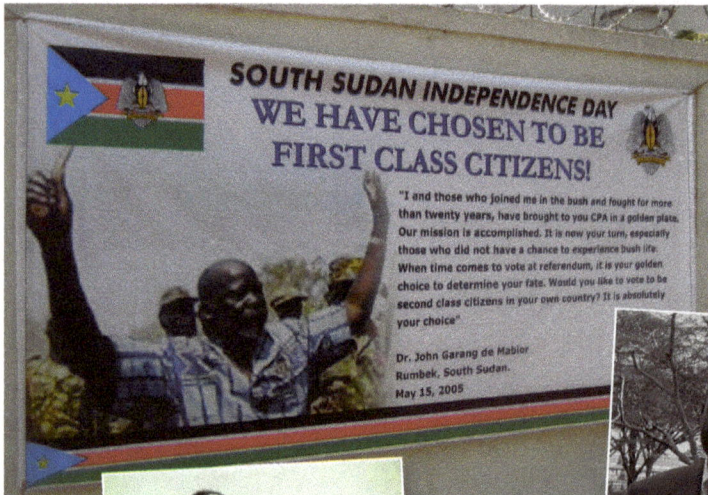

Figure 14: Poster showing John Garang campaigning for independence for South Sudan

Figure 15: John Garang with his wife, Rebecca (Photo credit: Aubrey Fagon)

Figure 16: John Garang speaking at Iowa State University

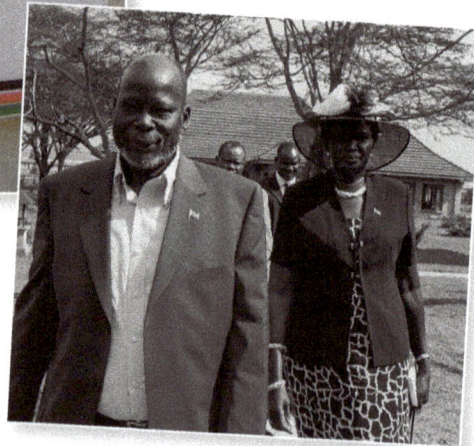

South Sudan

South Sudan became an independent nation at midnight on 9 July 2011 after the January 2011 referendum passed. Around ninety-nine per cent of voters were in favour of the split. South Sudan mainly voted to be separate from Sudan because of cultural and religious differences.

South Sudan is the world's newest country. It is on the continent of Africa to the south of Sudan. It covers 619,745 square kilometres (239,285 square miles).

It has an estimated population of eleven million.

The capital of South Sudan is Juba (population 403,000). South Sudan borders Ethiopia, Kenya, Uganda, the Democratic Republic of the Congo, Central African Republic and Sudan.

The Government of South Sudan

South Sudan's interim constitution was ratified on 7 July 2011. It has a presidential system of government. President Salva Kiir Mayardit is the head of the government. It has three historical provinces (Bahr el Ghazal, Equatoria and Greater Upper Nile) and Juba is its capital city, which is in the state of Central Equatoria.

Industry

The main products in South Sudan are cotton, sugarcane, wheat, nuts, and fruit such mangoes, papaya and bananas.

Geography and climate

South Sudan is a landlocked country in eastern Africa. Its landscape consists of tropical rainforest. Its protected national parks are home to much migrating wildlife. South Sudan also has extensive swamp and grassland regions. The White Nile, a main tributary of the Nile River, passes through the country.

The highest point in South Sudan is Kinyeti, at 3,187 metres (10,456 feet), located on its far southern border with Uganda.

The climate of South Sudan is mainly tropical.

Juba, the capital and largest city in South Sudan, has an average yearly high temperature of 34.5°C (94.1°F). Its average yearly low temperature is 21.6°C (70.9°F). Most of the rainfall occurs between April and October. The average yearly total rainfall is 953.7 millimetres (37.54 inches).

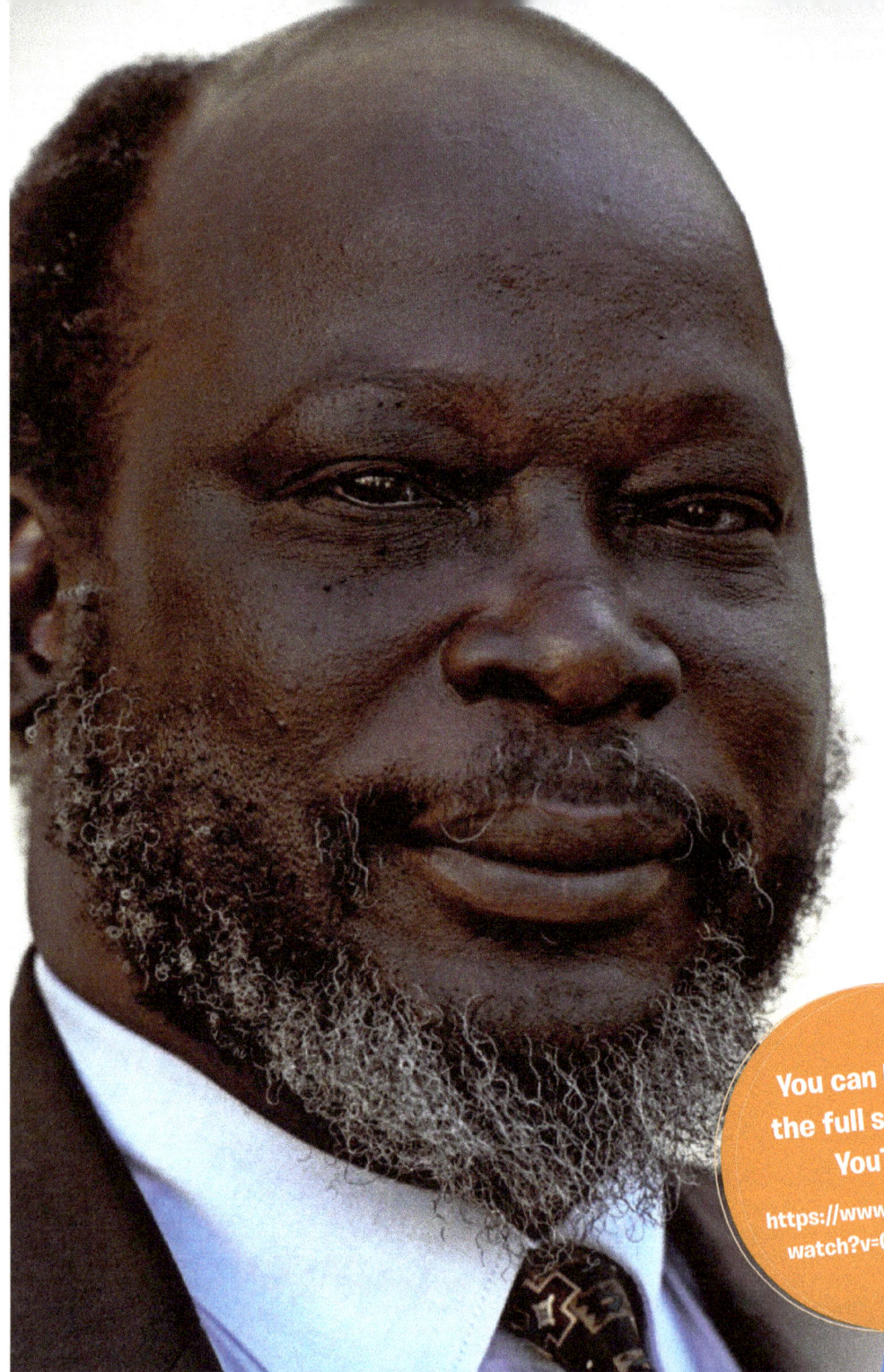

You can listen to the full speech on YouTube:

https://www.youtube.com/watch?v=GfnhnDeUgpQ

PART 2

Dr John Garang made a famous speech at the signing ceremony of the South Sudan peace deal on 9 January 2005.

The second part of this book is a summary of that speech.

Dr Garang used his speech to tell all Sudanese people that the signing of the peace deal meant a united Sudan. He said the country could be split if working together didn't work. His movement would try to preserve Sudan as one nation.

2005 year of peace

Dr Garang called 2005 the year of peace for the whole of Sudan, and throughout Africa.

He greeted all Sudanese people from Nimule in the far south to Halfa in the far north, and from Geneinah in the far west to Hamashkoreb and Port Sudan in the east. He greeted all rural people, women, farmers, workers, students and professionals.

He described how hard Sudanese rural woman work. They get up at five o'clock in the morning to walk five kilometres to get five gallons (19 litres) of water. They spend another five hours working on the family farm. They spend five more hours making the family meal.

He urged students and young people to invest in their future and that of the nation.

Figure 17: Dr Garang with United Nations Secretary General Kofi (Photo Source: www.thoughtco.com - Spencer Platt / Staff / Getty Images)

Figure 18: Dr Garang with Nelson Mandela

The second republic of the new Sudan

With this peace agreement, he said, the longest war in Africa had ended. Sudan had been at war with itself for 49 years.

The peace agreement meant there would be no more bombs falling from the sky on innocent children and women. Instead, children would giggle happily.

Dr Garang said that the unity of Sudan would be based on the free will of the people instead of on the wars of the last 49 years.

This peace agreement would begin the process of achieving independence by all Sudanese people and for all Sudanese people.

This peace agreement was the beginning of the new Sudan. He said:

> From here on Sudan for the first time will be a country voluntarily united in justice, honour and dignity for all its citizens regardless of their race, regardless of their religion, regardless of their gender.

Dr Garang called on the Sudanese people to join the peace agreement. He said it 'belongs to all of Sudan, to its neighbours, to Africa, to the Arab world and to the rest of the world'.

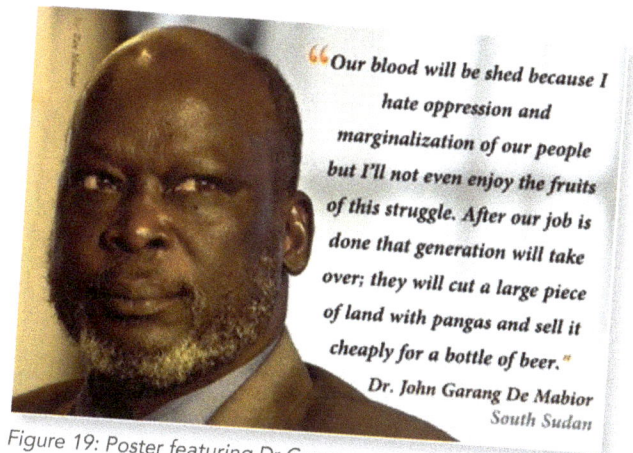

"Our blood will be shed because I hate oppression and marginalization of our people but I'll not even enjoy the fruits of this struggle. After our job is done that generation will take over; they will cut a large piece of land with pangas and sell it cheaply for a bottle of beer."

Dr. John Garang De Mabior
South Sudan

Figure 19: Poster featuring Dr Garang

Tribute to heroes; release of prisoners of war

Dr Garang paid tribute to all the wounded heroes on both sides of the war. He congratulated all the soldiers. He thanked the civil population for their help. He said without their contribution the peace agreement would not have been possible.

He also talked about prisoners of war:

On this joyous occasion of the signing of the comprehensive peace agreement ... I here as of today order the immediate release of all prisoners of war that are still under the custody and care of the SPLA.

Tsunami victims

At the end of 2004, one of the world's deadliest natural disasters killed more than 200,000 people in Asia and Africa. It was caused by a huge earthquake in the Indian Ocean. The earthquake caused a tsunami.

Dr Garang said:

Our hearts go out in grief and solidarity to the peoples of southeast Asia in this their hour of tragedy in the hands of a merciless earthquake and tsunami. As we share the pain and suffering of our fellow human beings in all the countries that have been devastated ... we also urge the international community, after it has pledged so generously to help alleviate the suffering and rebuild shattered lives in the affected region, to spare some resources to help post-conflict Sudan recover and develop.

An all-inclusive Sudanese state

Dr Garang then went on to talk about the problem the SPLM wanted to solve now. He said that while the current war was ending, there were other conflicts.

The problem was caused by previous governments trying to build an Arab Islamic state. This government left out most of the southern Sudanese people.

The people who were left out resisted. Wars would continue if the majority of Sudanese people were not included in governing Sudan.

He proposed a new Sudan, with all Sudanese people equal in the eyes of the government, whatever their religion, race, tribe or gender. It would only be if that didn't work that splitting the country would be considered.

But we believe that a new Sudan is possible for there are many people in northern Sudan who share with us in SPLM/A, including the National Congress Party, who believe in the universal ideals of humanity, the ideals of liberty, of freedom, justice and equality, of opportunity for all Sudanese citizens.

He added that this all-inclusive Sudanese state must have something in common to make it one country. He believed that the history of the people would make this possible.

Move forward with the momentum of 5,000 years

He suggested that Sudanese people remember their thousands of years of history so they could gain the momentum to move forward.

He talked about the Old Testament in the Bible. Genesis Chapter 2, Verses 8 to 14 states that Sudan was part of the Garden of Eden. The Garden of Eden was watered by four rivers, the White Nile, the Blue Nile the Tigris and the Euphrates. That means it covered a large area.

Ancient Sudanese kingdoms relate to the present-day Dinka, Shiluk, Nuer and other Nilotic tribes.

Sudanese history progressed from the Islamic kingdoms of Sinar to the Teko Egyptian occupation. Anglo-Egyptian independence in 1956 was followed by the Anya Nya movement from 1955 to 1972. This led to the SPLM/SPLA in 1983.

Sudanese history has been a long journey of more than 5,000 years. Only by knowing and appreciating from 'where we came' can we 'better chart the way forward,' said Dr Garang.

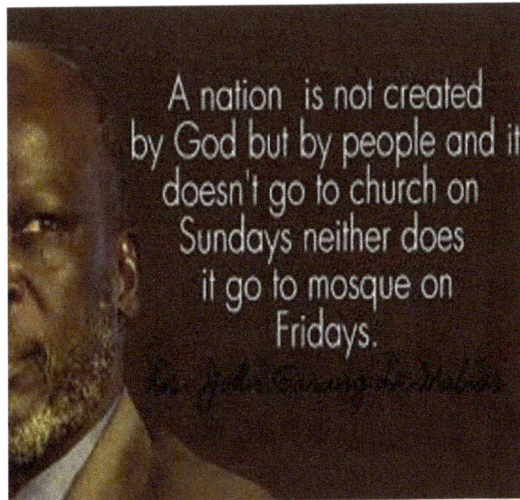

Figure 20: Poster featuring Dr Garang

National unity through democracy

There are more than 500 ethnic groups speaking more than 130 languages in Sudan. There are two major religions – Islam and Christianity – as well as traditional African religions. Dr Garang said he believed that 'Sudan's history, diversity and richness is the common heritage of all Sudanese.' This heritage formed the basis of the peace agreement.

He assured people from the north that the SPLM would work with the National Congress Party to keep the country together.

Dr Garang said human rights and people's rights would be protected in the constitution. The court system would be upheld. An independent civil service would be established.

The peace agreement meant that within three to four years people would participate in internationally monitored free and fair elections.

Figure 21: Dr Garang with Colin Powell and various dignitaries
EPA/STEPHEN MORRISON

Figure 22:
Dr Garang with
Humanitarian
Dr. Bob Arnot

Economic and social development

Dr Garang recognised that economic changes would not fix the nation's problems, but would help address the current problems.

He spoke of child malnutrition, lack of primary education, child and maternal death rates, and access to improved water sources. Statistics on these areas in southern Sudan were among the worst in the world. The SPLM strategic framework set out a social, political and economic development strategy.

There would be growth in rural development through technological innovations. Crop production would be guaranteed by building dykes for flood control. Canals and underground water would be developed for irrigation.

Development would be decentralised rather than centralised in cities and towns:

The SPLM ... will take the towns to people in the countryside rather than people to towns, where they end up in slums.

The framework emphasised the development of new ways of delivering social services. Health, education and water needed immediate attention. The SPLM would build windmills all over rural Sudan to provide clean drinking water. Micro-dams would generate small-scale hydro-electric power for rural towns. Solar, wind and bio-gas energy sources would be used.

Roads, rail and river transport and telecommunications were also on the agenda.

Finally, he said, the SPLM would restore the dignity of the people of the Sudan. Programs would include:

information and media, radio, TV, print, promotion of new Sudan art, songs, dances, theatre of new Sudan, sports, development of local languages and cultures by the various communities of the Sudan, archives of the struggle and modern history of Sudan, archaeology, antiquities and ancient history of Sudan, Africa and the Middle East so that we can find our rightful place in the world.

Building national consensus

Dr Garang pledged that the SPLM would work in partnership with the National Congress Party. Together they would implement the peace agreement and provide permanent solutions to Sudan's problems.

He stressed the positives of diversity as a source of national cohesion and strength. 'Viewed otherwise', he said, would lead 'to the ultimate disintegration of the country,' which must be avoided. Political struggle in Sudan would become competing visions of peace and development, rather than the use of force.

Dr Garang expressed hope for national consensus, and said the exclusion of anybody from this process would not be tolerated.

Dr Garang called on the political parties within the National Congress Party and the National Democratic Alliance to complete negotiations with the government of Sudan.

He also appealed to those who had left Sudan to return home and participate in the development of southern Sudan.

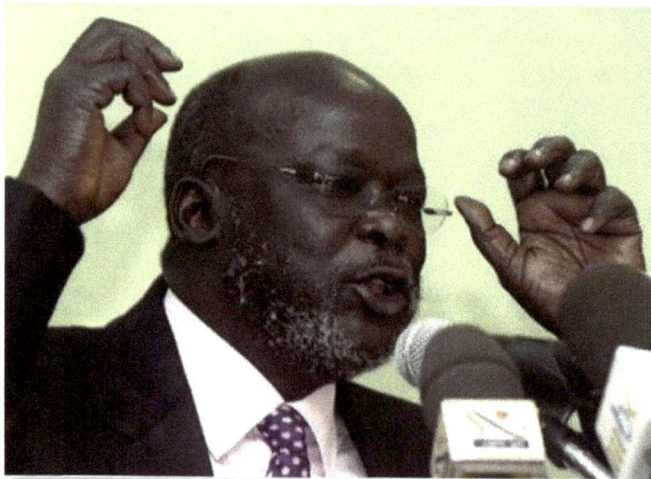

Figure 23: Dr Garang speaking at the signing ceremony of the South Sudan peace deal

Tributes and acknowledgements

Dr Garang paid tribute to the fallen heroes on both sides of the conflict.

He saluted the courage of President Umar Hasan al-Bashir and Ustadh Ali Uthman Taha for negotiating the peace agreement. He thanked the people of east Africa, the Horn, the Arab world and the international community. On many occasions, he said, they either volunteered to help bring peace to Sudan or encouraged the peace process.

He also thanked the many presidents of other countries for their contribution to the Sudan peace process.

To finish his speech, he said:

I pay tribute and thanks to my dear wife Rebecca and the wives of all my colleagues and comrades in the struggle for their patience and contributions, for without their help the bush would not have been bearable .... I pay tribute finally to all the Sudanese people, to whom this peace belongs, and I say to them mobruk ol lekum [congratulations].

Figure 24: Rebecca Garang

References

Briney, Amanda. (3 March 2011). "Geography of Sudan - Learn the Geography of the African Nation of Sudan." Geography at About.com. Retrieved from: http://geography.about.com/od/sudanmaps/a/sudan-geography.htm

British Broadcasting Company. (8 July 2011). "South Sudan Becomes an Independent Nation." BBC News Africa. Retrieved from: http://www.bbc.co.uk/news/world-africa-14089843 Goffard, Christopher. (10 July 2011). "South Sudan: New Nation of South Sudan Declares Independence."

http://www.latimes.com/news/nationworld/world/la-fg-south-sudan-independence-20110710,0,2964065.story

Wikipedia.org. (10 July 2011). South Sudan - Wikipedia, the Free Encyclopedia. Retrieved from: http://en.wikipedia.org/wiki/South_Sudan

Image References

Cover Note	Used with Permission: St Columba College, South Australia
Foreword	Shutterstock Stock Image, Purchased with Standard License
Part 1	Shutterstock Stock Image, Purchased with Standard License
Figure 1	https://www.pinterest.com.au/pin/550916966894415140/
Figure 2.1	https://www.facebook.com/246829412625733/posts/dr-john-garang-de-mabiori-have-been-commanding-the-spla-officiers-and-men-of-var/652604828714854/
Figure 2.2	http://furahaamon.blogspot.com/2014/02/kifo-cha-john-garang.html
Figure 3.1	Source unknown
Figure 3.2	https://www.facebook.com/509784539095170/posts/biography-of-the-late-dr-john-garang-de-mabiorjune-23-1945-july-30-2005founding-/3909872429086347/
Figure 4	Source unknown
Figure 5	https://www.facebook.com/thevisionforchange/photos/dr-john-garang-and-his-family-a-true-revolutionary-was-a-simple-man-just-like-an/10151049203298983/
Figure 6	https://ar-ar.facebook.com/pg/johngarang91/photos/
Figure 7	https://www.facebook.com/pg/John.JohnGarang/photos/
Figure 8	https://www.facebook.com/pg/Dr-John-Garang-1895101524062560/posts/
Figure 9	https://twitter.com/mosestut?lang=en
Figure 10	https://paanluelwel.com/2018/07/30/tears-of-hopelessness-the-painful-experience-after-john-garang-death/
Figure 11	http://www.bbc.co.uk/french/highlights/story/2005/12/051231_afrique_2005.shtml
Figure 12	http://news.bbc.co.uk/2/hi/in_pictures/4735725.stm
Figure 13	https://commons.wikimedia.org/wiki/File:Rebecca_Nyandeng_De_Mabior_with_George_Bush_February_10,_2006.jpg
Figure 14	https://internallydisplaced.wordpress.com/tag/independence-day/
Figure 15	Photo provided with permission, Aubrey Fagon https://aubz.co.uk/south-sudan-2004
Figure 16	Source unknown

Image References cont.

Part 2	http://rudebutgood.blogspot.com/2012/02/john-garang.html
Figure 17	https://www.thoughtco.com/john-garang-de-mabior-43576
Figure 18	Adobe Stock - Standard Licence
Figure 19	https://twitter.com/JunobJ/status/1148230153463619584
Figure 20	Source unknown
Figure 21.1	https://midtifleisen.wordpress.com/2018/12/26/alt-vi-vet-om-delingen-av-sudan-er-uriktig-intervju-med-michel-raimbaud/ https://eyeradio.org/kenya-calls-for-timely-formation-of-coalition-government/"
Figure 21.2	http://johngarangvision.blogspot.com/2008/08/drjohn-garang-s-quotes.html"
Figure 22	https://al.nd.edu/news/latest-news/liberal-arts-education-inspires-life-of-learning/
Figure 23	https://panafricanvisions.com/2013/03/dr-john-garangs-forgotten-2004-message-a-wake-up-call-for-south-sudanese-diaspora/
Figure 23	https://eagle.co.ug/2017/12/20/rebecca-garang-wants-south-sudan-president-salva-kiir-ousted.html